Heart
and
Lungs

JANE SAUNDERSON

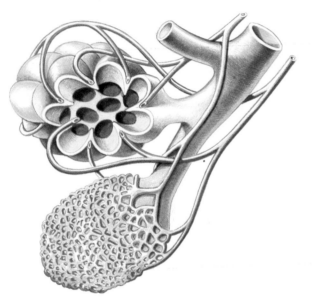

illustrated by
ANDREW FARMER and **ROBINA GREEN**

Troll Associates

Library of Congress Cataloging-in-Publication Data

Saunderson, Jane.
    Heart and lungs / written by Jane Saunderson; illustrated by Andrew
Farmer & Robina Green.
        p.   cm.
    Summary: Describes the workings of the human cardiopulmonary
system.
    ISBN 0-8167-2096-7 (lib. bdg.)   ISBN 0-8167-2097-5 (pbk.)
    1. Cardiopulmonary system—Physiology—Juvenile literature.
[1. Cardiopulmonary system.   2. Heart.   3. Lungs.]   I. Farmer,
Andrew, ill.   II. Green, Robina, ill.   III. Title.
QP103.S28 1992
612.1—dc20   90-42881

Published by Troll Associates.

Copyright © 1992 Eagle Books Limited

Edited by Neil Morris
Designed by COOPER-WILSON
Picture research by Jan Croot

Printed in the U.S.A.

10   9   8   7   6   5   4   3   2   1

Illustrators

Andrew Farmer front and back cover, pp 1, 2, 3, 4,
    6, 9, 10, 11, 12-13, 14-15, 15, 17, 18, 20, 22-23
Robina Green front cover, pp 5, 12, 24, 25, 26,
    28, 29

Additional illustrations by COOPER-WILSON

Picture credits:
Science Photo Library front cover, 27 (top), (CNRI)
    7, 13, 19, 24, (Gary Settles) II, (NIBSC) 22,
    (Astrid and Hans-Frieder Michler) 27 (bottom)

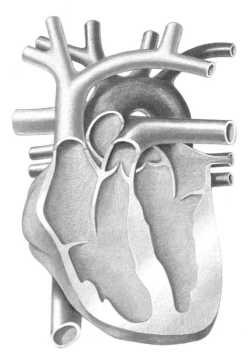

Contents

Why do you need your heart and lungs?

You are a living being made of millions of tiny particles called *cells*. All cells share similar features, but the exact design and size of a cell depends on what job it does, and where it is in the body. Cells group themselves into different patterns to form *tissues* of your body.

Here are two examples of cells found in your body: *Nerve cells* that carry messages between the brain and the rest of the body are different from the *epithelial cells* lining your stomach, which produce juices to help you digest food.

▶ Cells need food and oxygen. Your lungs guide oxygen into the bloodstream. Your heart pumps blood around the body, delivering food and oxygen to cells.

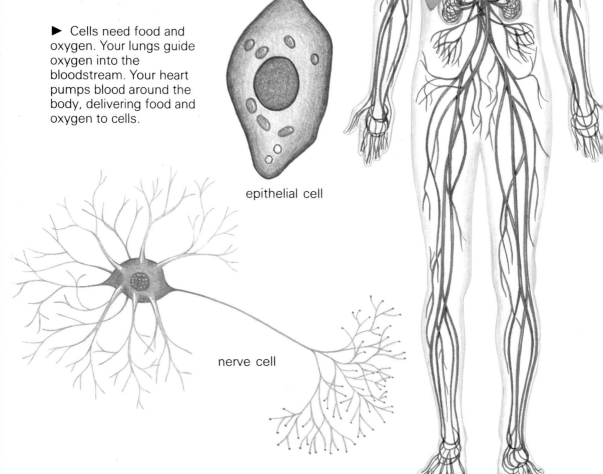

epithelial cell

nerve cell

You have millions and millions of cells in your body! These cells are active and need food to produce energy. They make energy by burning food, with the help of oxygen. Oxygen is the essential fuel needed for all the chemical reactions that take place in the body, in the same way that gasoline is the essential fuel for a car.

You live on a planet that has an atmosphere rich in oxygen. How does the food you have eaten, and the oxygen you breathe in, get to where they are needed? The answer lies in your heart and lungs.

When you breathe in, air containing oxygen travels down into your lungs. Here the oxygen is guided into your bloodstream and swapped for carbon dioxide, a waste gas. Carbon dioxide leaves your body as you breathe out.

Your heart and blood vessels form your body's major transportation system. Your heart pumps blood around your body through miles (kilometers) of blood vessels. The blood delivers food and oxygen to cells all over your body. It also takes waste matter away from cells.

▲ Running takes more energy than sitting reading. When you run, your body cells need more oxygen, so you breathe faster and your heart pumps faster.

5

Air and your lungs

The air you breathe is made up of different gases. About 21 percent of air is oxygen, the gas your cells need most. Air also contains nitrogen (about 78 percent), plus tiny amounts of argon, carbon dioxide, and other gases.

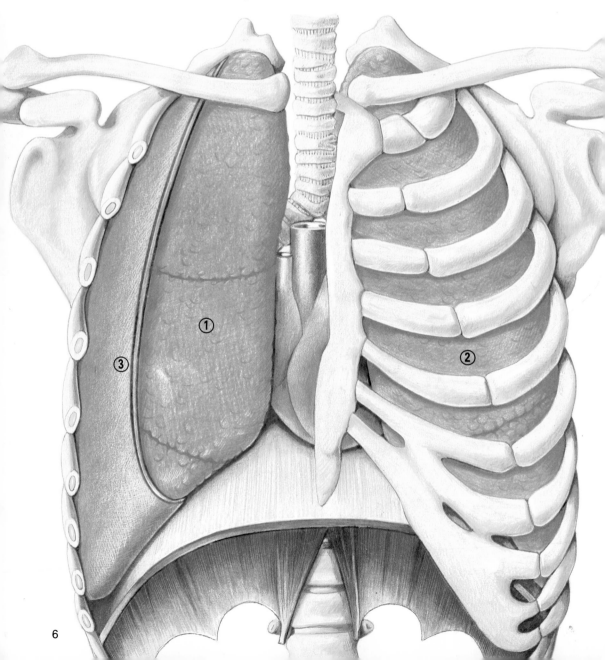

Trees and plants also breathe. During daylight hours they breathe in carbon dioxide and breathe out oxygen. This helps to keep a healthy balance of gases in our planet's atmosphere.

1 The lung on your right side has three compartments or *lobes*.

2 The lung on your left has only two lobes, to make room for your heart, which snuggles in between your lungs.

3 Your lungs are attached to the inside of your rib cage by a two-layered, airtight "skin" called the *pleura*. The *visceral* layer covers the outer surface of your lungs. The *parietal* layer attaches to your rib cage. Between these two layers of the pleura there is a small amount of thick fluid. This allows the layers to slide easily against each other as you breathe.

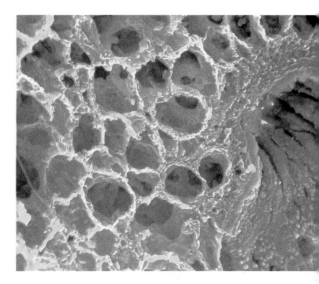

You breathe air into your lungs through many damp air passages. But lungs are not hollow. They are like elastic sponges, containing millions of tiny air sacs, called *alveoli*. If these sacs could be spread out flat, they would cover about half a tennis court!

Lungs are large, filling most of your rib cage. Altogether the lungs weigh about two pounds (one kilogram).

▲ A magnified photo of a section of a lung, showing alveoli. They are surrounded by tiny blood vessels. Air reaches the alveoli through passages called bronchioles. You can see a bronchiole at the right of the photo.

How air gets into your lungs

The heart and lungs in your chest are separated from the organs in your *abdomen*, such as the stomach, liver, and intestines, by a large dome of muscle called the *diaphragm*. Stretching from your backbone to the front and sides of your rib cage, this is the main muscle for breathing. It is attached to the bottom of your lungs by the pleura. A hiccup is caused by your diaphragm contracting more strongly than usual.

In between your ribs are smaller muscles which help your chest move in and out. These are called *intercostal* muscles.

When you breathe in, the intercostal muscles contract, which pulls the ribs up and out. At the same time, the diaphragm contracts and flattens. Both these actions stretch the lung

▼ Air is drawn into your lungs (*left*), as your rib cage expands and your diaphragm flattens. When you breathe out (*right*), your ribs move inward and your diaphragm rises.

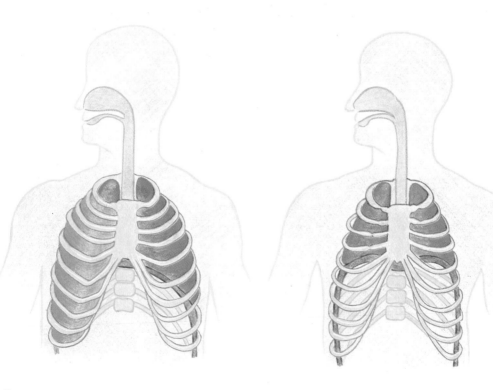

tissue and make the space inside your chest larger. As your lungs expand, the air pressure inside them lowers. Air rushes in from the outside to balance the pressure.

When you breathe out, the intercostal muscles and diaphragm relax. Your ribs move in and the diaphragm rises, making the space inside your chest smaller. Your stretchy lungs return to their previous size, the pressure inside them increases, and air is pushed out.

How many times have you breathed in and out since you started reading this page? Most of the time we are unaware of breathing. An adult may breathe in and out more than 20,000 times a day. Breathing is controlled by the lower part of our brain, which looks after many things our bodies do automatically. The brain constantly checks how much oxygen and carbon dioxide are in our bloodstream. If we have too little oxygen, or too much carbon dioxide, our brain sends a message along the nerves to tell the breathing muscles to make us breathe faster.

When you run, your body cells need more oxygen, so you breathe faster. When you go to sleep, the cells need less oxygen, so you breathe more slowly. Sometimes if we get anxious or frightened, we gasp and hold our breath. If you find yourself doing this, relax and let your chest work freely.

▼ The brain is the body's control center. The top part of the brain has folds and grooves on the outside. Many things happen here: you think, store memories, understand speech and hearing, control movement, feel sensations, and much more. The lower, stalklike part of the brain controls many automatic things that your body does, including how fast you breathe.

Your nose

Most of the time you breathe through your nose. Your nose has two nostrils, with a *septum*, or wall, between them. Sometimes we have to breathe through our mouths. Our nose may be blocked because of a cold, or if we are exercising hard we may need more oxygen than our nose can take in. But these are exceptions – your nose was designed to be the place where air begins its journey to your lungs, because it does many useful jobs.

▼ Your nose moistens, cleans, and warms incoming air. The olfactory nerve on the roof of your nose enables you to smell. If your nose is tickled, you may sneeze to clear the passages.

Moisture control. If incoming air is not moist enough, the lining wall of your nose produces a sticky mucus that helps to moisten the air. Otherwise, the air passages to your lungs will dry out.

Cleaning the air. Your nose provides a cleaning service for incoming air. Hairs at the entrance filter out particles of dirt. Smaller particles get stuck to the mucus and are brought to the entrance of your nose, or to your throat to be swallowed. All this is done by hundreds of little hairs, called *cilia*, that line the walls deep inside your nose.

Temperature control. In your nose, incoming air is warmed to your body temperature (98.6°F, 37°C) so it will not hurt your lungs. When you breathe gently, air enters your nose at just under four miles (about six kilometers) per hour.

Smell. When you smell such things as roses or cheese, tiny scent particles travel into your nose with the air. They dissolve in the mucous lining of the nose. A message is then sent by the *olfactory nerve* to your brain, which recognizes the smell.

Sneezing. When you have a cold or hay fever, your nose gets blocked. The lining of your nose swells and produces too much mucus, so air can't get in. If the lining wall is tickled or gets irritated, it reacts by making you sneeze. A powerful sneeze can reach a speed between 37 and 100 miles (60 and 160 kilometers) per hour! It helps clear your nose of unwanted particles.

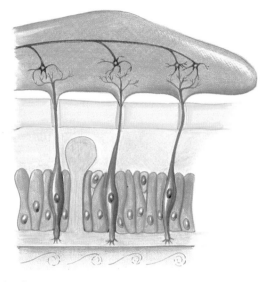

▲ Scent particles dissolve in the mucous lining. They stimulate the olfactory nerve, which sends a message to your brain. This is how you smell.

▼ When you sneeze, air, mucus, and particles are explosively expelled.

Your throat

After passing through your nose, air travels through your throat on the next stage of its journey to your lungs.

1 From your nose the air moves down into the top part of your throat, called the *pharynx*. This part of the throat is used both for breathing and by food on its way to your stomach.

2 A little further down, the tube divides. The air continues its journey into the lower part of your throat, the *larynx*. Food travels down the *esophagus* (**7**) into your stomach.

3 When you swallow, a flap called the *epiglottis* closes like a trap door over the entrance to the larynx. This makes sure the food goes down the right tube and doesn't follow the air into your lungs. Sometimes a piece of food goes down "the wrong way," into the larynx. This irritates the lining of the larynx, which makes you cough to get rid of the unwanted visitor.

▲ The vocal cords. When the cords are apart, air can pass freely and no sound is made. Tiny muscles pull the cords together, leaving a small gap. As air is forced through this gap, it makes the cords vibrate and sounds are made.

4 Put your fingers on your Adam's apple, which is at the front of your larynx. Can you feel it move up as you swallow and the epiglottis closes?

5 The larynx is also your "voice box." Two soft folds called *vocal cords* open and close across the tube. As air passes over the vocal cords, sounds are made.

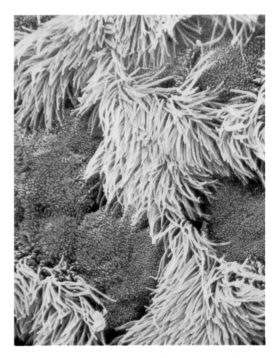

▲ The windpipe is lined with hairlike strands called cilia.

6 The air continues into your windpipe, or *trachea*, and moves deep inside your chest. The walls of the trachea are covered with hundreds of tiny cilia. Other cells in the wall make a sticky mucus which traps any remaining dirt. The cilia move the mucus upward to be swallowed.

13

Inside your lungs

At the bottom of your windpipe, the air passage divides just below the middle of your breastbone. One tube, or *bronchus*, leads to the left lung and the other to the right lung. Inside each lung, the bronchus divides into hundreds of smaller passages, rather like the branches of a tree.

▲ The bronchus (**1**) and large blood vessels (**2**) enter the lung at the same point. The bronchus divides into smaller passages called bronchioles (**3**).

► The smallest air passages in the lungs end in tiny sacs called alveoli. These are covered in a fine mesh of blood vessels. Here oxygen passes into the blood vessels, and carbon dioxide passes from them.

These smaller passages are called *bronchioles*. Their walls contain a layer of muscle that can make the bronchioles narrower or wider.

The passages get smaller and smaller, until they eventually open out into many little balloon-like sacs called alveoli. Their walls are very thin and contain no muscle. The outer surface of the alveoli is covered with many tiny blood vessels called *capillaries*.

Lungs are made of hundreds of tiny air passages and about three hundred million alveoli. Elastic tissue between the alveoli supports them and allows them to stretch as we breathe in and out.

Oxygen particles from the air seep through the walls of the alveoli into the blood vessels. Each particle of oxygen attaches to a red blood cell and is taken to the heart. As the blood collects its oxygen, it passes carbon dioxide to the alveoli, so that it can be breathed out of the body.

Your heart

Once blood has collected oxygen from your lungs, the blood circulates back to your heart. Your heart lies in your chest, just to the left of the bottom of your breastbone. It is well protected by the rib cage. The heart is pear-shaped and about the size of your fist.

Every part of your body needs a regular supply of blood. Your heart makes sure it gets there. Each day the heart pumps about 7,200 quarts (7,500 liters) of blood around the body.

The heart is made of *cardiac muscle*, a special type of muscle found only in the heart. The heart works rather like two pumps sitting side by side. The left and the right sides of the heart are divided by a muscular wall called a *septum*. The right side collects blood carrying waste carbon dioxide from the body, and pumps it to the lungs, so that we can breathe it out. The left side of your heart collects blood with fresh oxygen from the lungs, which it pumps out into the body.

A heartbeat is one complete contraction and relaxation of the heart muscle, which usually takes less than one second. Fortunately you don't have to remember to make your heart beat. An area of cells in the right atrium called the *pacemaker* sends impulses out through the heart muscle, which responds by contracting and then relaxing. The lower part of your brain influences your heartbeat. It does this by sending messages to the pacemaker, instructing it to speed up or slow down your heartbeat.

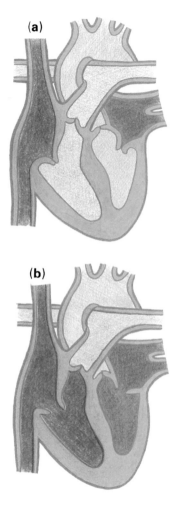

(a)

(b)

▲ The action of the heart. (**a**) Blood flows into the two atria. (**b**) The atria contract and push blood down into the ventricles. (**c**) Valves close to stop blood running back into the atria. (**d**) The ventricles contract and push blood to your lungs and all parts of your body.

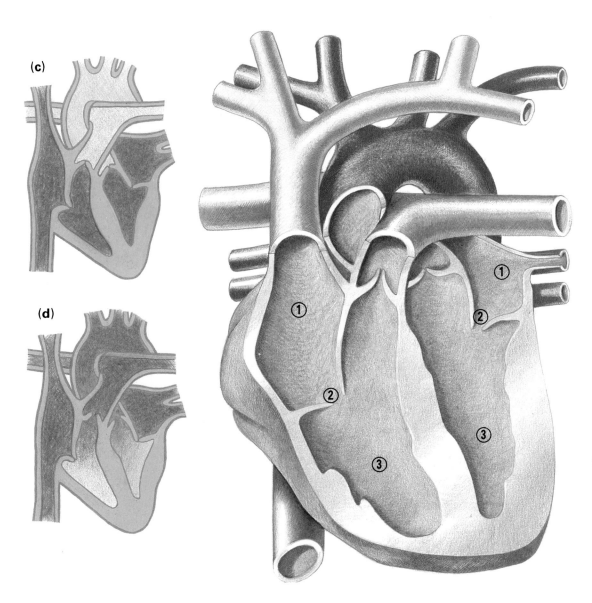

(c)

(d)

1 Each side of the heart has an *atrium*, or upper chamber, where blood is collected from the veins.

2 The upper and lower chambers are divided by a valve. The valve allows only one-way traffic between the chambers. This means that blood can flow down, but not back up.

3 Blood flowing through the valve from the atrium enters the *ventricle*, or lower chamber. The ventricles form the largest part of the heart, and their thick, strong muscular walls contract to pump blood into your *arteries*. Because the left ventricle must pump blood to all parts of your body, its walls are even thicker than those of the right ventricle.

Arteries and capillaries

Blood travels around your body through about 100,000 miles (160,000 kilometers) of blood vessels.

Let's trace its journey, starting in the left ventricle of your heart and going down to your toes.

1 Blood looks bright red when it is carrying oxygen. As it leaves your heart, the oxygen-rich blood is carried to the rest of your body in thick muscular blood vessels called arteries.

2 The first artery the blood travels through is also the largest. It is called the *aorta*, and it branches out into smaller and smaller arteries that reach every part of the body.

3 Some blood enters the artery that branches off to the liver. Your liver has many different jobs to do. It is a storehouse for vitamins and for energy-giving starch and glucose. The liver releases these substances into the bloodstream when you need them. It also breaks down worn-out cells and processes fats and proteins.

4 More blood takes a route to the kidneys. These small organs clean all of your blood every fifty minutes. They remove waste chemicals and some water from the blood to make *urine*.

5 Another artery branches off to the *small intestine*. Digested food from the small intestine seeps into the bloodstream, which then transports it all around your body.

6 Just below your waist, the aorta divides into two arteries, one leading to each of your legs. As they branch off into smaller, narrower vessels, they become so small the red blood cells move through them in single file. These tiny vessels are called capillaries. It is through the thin walls of the capillaries that oxygen and food seep from your bloodstream into all your cells, to keep them growing and healthy.

▲ A photo of densely-packed red blood cells moving through a capillary. The photo is magnified over 2,500 times.

Having lost its oxygen, the blood turns a dusty, brownish red. Now it is ready for the climb back to your heart.

Veins

Just as a car gives off exhaust fumes, so the chemical processes in your body produce carbon dioxide and other waste materials. These seep back into your bloodstream. The vessels that carry blood on its return journey to the heart are called *veins*. We have more veins than arteries.

Let's follow the blood on its way back to the right atrium of your heart.

1 Having picked up its carbon dioxide, the blood travels back through the capillaries. These get wider, until the blood reaches a vein. A vein is large, like an artery, but has a thinner muscle wall.

2 Deep inside your body, the veins get larger and larger as they join with other veins bringing blood back from various parts of your body.

3 Eventually, the blood returning with carbon dioxide from your big toe finds itself in the right atrium of your heart. From there it flows into the right ventricle, where it will be pumped to the lungs, to begin its journey all over again.

It is hard for the blood to travel back to your heart because it has to flow against gravity. The pumping of the heart is not enough, so your body has other ways to help the blood on its return journey.

There are little flaps called *valves* in many of the veins. These stop the blood from flowing backward.

As you move, the muscles around your veins contract. This squeezes the veins and helps push the blood onward.

As you breathe in, your chest increases in size, which helps draw the blood upward.

This is why a brisk walk can help improve your circulation.

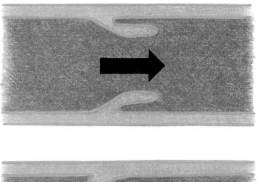

◀ Veins in the lower part of your body have little flaps called valves inside them. These allow blood to flow upward toward the heart, but close to prevent it from flowing backward. As you move, your muscles contract. This puts pressure on the veins and helps squeeze the blood toward your heart.

Blood

When you are grown, you will have about five quarts (5 liters) of blood in your body. When you are sitting still, the blood's trip from your heart around your body and back to your heart takes about a minute.

About 35 percent of your blood is made up of cells and disklike substances called *platelets*. A tiny drop of blood contains about 6½ million cells floating in a clear yellow liquid, called *plasma*. If you put some blood in a glass jar, it would divide into two parts. The solids would sink to the bottom, leaving the plasma on top.

Your blood contains two different kinds of cells. Each kind of cell does a different job.

▲ A photo taken by an electron microscope of a red cell, white cell, and platelet, magnified over 1,000 times.

1 *Red cells* give blood its color. They are made by red bone marrow. Red blood cells deliver oxygen to and remove carbon dioxide from your body. After about 120 days they wear out and are destroyed. They are reddest when they are carrying oxygen. Red cells are the most numerous of your blood cells. There are about 6 million in a tiny drop of blood.

2 *White cells* are not really white, but colorless. They are generally larger than red cells, but we have fewer of them. There are about 10,000 in a tiny drop of blood. White cells are the body's defenders, and they come in many types. While some help protect us from infection, others fight unwanted organisms that have gotten into our bodies.

3 Platelets are the smallest parts of the blood. There are about 400,000 in a tiny drop of blood. If you cut yourself, platelets will stick together to plug any leaks in the blood vessel.

The other 65 per cent of your blood is plasma, which carries lots of vital things around your body. Digested foods such as fat, sugar, and salt are transported from your digestive system to all the cells in your body. Proteins, which are important to help your blood clot if you cut yourself, are circulated. Waste products are transported to the liver and kidneys. These are just a few of the jobs plasma does for you.

Any questions?

How often does my heart beat?

When an adult is sitting quietly, his or her heart may beat about 70 times a minute – that means about 100,000 times a day! But when you are active, your cells need more oxygen and food, so your heart beats faster. If you are running fast, it may beat more than 150 times a minute. These changes in your heart rate are controlled by your brain.

You can measure your pulse rate by putting the fingers on your wrist below your thumb, and pressing gently. You'll feel the blood pulsing through the artery in your wrist. Count how many beats you feel in one minute. That's your heart rate.

What happens when I cut myself?

You break the wall of a blood vessel. Blood starts to escape and you bleed. The body naturally wants to stop the flow of blood, so it sets an emergency procedure into operation.

Other substances in the plasma set to work forming strands of protein. These weave a web over the cut that traps platelets and blood cells to form a clot, which stops the bleeding. A blood clot on the surface of the skin is called a *scab*.

If you bump yourself and a blood vessel gets broken, but the blood doesn't come through your skin, you get a bruise.

▶ Strands of protein weave a web to form a clot.

Why are bruises blue?

If tiny blood vessels break, blood seeps into your skin tissues. *Hemoglobin*, the main element in your red cells, turns blue without oxygen. Because the vessels have broken, no more oxygen can reach the tissue. As the hemoglobin breaks down, it turns yellow, until it is removed by white blood cells. In about two weeks the bruise will disappear.

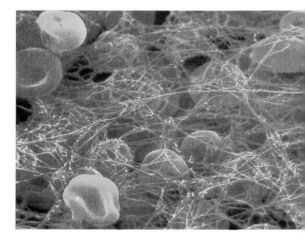

Why does the doctor tap my chest?

By placing the fingers of one hand on your skin and tapping them with the fingers of the other hand, the doctor can listen to your chest. Doctors tap in various spots, and on your back as well, to detect any abnormal sound their tapping makes. Healthy lungs sound hollow. If the air sacs in a lung are enlarged by disease, the sound will be even hollower. But if the lung contains fluid, or if it is collapsed, the tapping will produce a dull sound.

How does my blood help me when I'm hot?

Your blood helps to keep your body temperature at about 98.6°F (37°C). In hot weather, or after exercise, blood fills blood vessels near the surface of your skin. This helps your body to lose heat, and you get cooler. In cold weather, you need to keep warm, so the blood stays well below the surface.

What is blood pressure?

The force of blood pushing on the walls of the blood vessels is called blood pressure. A doctor can measure it with a machine called a *sphygmomanometer*. Having high blood pressure isn't painful, but it can harm your heart, as it has to work harder.

▲ A sphygmomanometer squeezes, but isn't painful. Your blood pressure is shown on the dial.

What can go wrong?

Most of us come into the world with a perfect set of heart and lungs. However, about one in a hundred babies is born with a slightly abnormal heart. Most of these *congenital*, or birth, defects cause no problems, but if they are more serious, an operation can usually correct them.

A few of us have diseases inherited from our parents. One such disease that affects the lungs is called *cystic fibrosis*. In this disease, the lungs produce very large amounts of sticky mucus that clog up the air passages.

As we grow older, some of us will be lucky and never have a serious illness that affects our heart or lungs. Unfortunately, some of us will. Let's look at three common problems.

▼ During an asthma attack, the air passages in the lungs get narrower, making breathing difficult. People who suffer from asthma often use an inhaler to breathe in a drug that helps open the air passages.

Asthma. When someone has asthma, the air passages in the lungs get narrower. The muscle layer in the wall of the air passages contracts, and the lining of the wall becomes swollen. A lot of extra mucus is produced. People with asthma find it difficult to breathe, especially to breathe out. As they try, they produce a wheezy sound and cough.

Chronic bronchitis. This is a serious disease which affects the lungs. One of the causes is cigarette smoking. The smoke causes damage to the air passages in the lungs. This makes the air passages produce more mucus than usual and become narrower. Air is difficult to draw through the damaged passages. People with this disease wheeze when they breathe, and get short of breath very easily.

Heart attack. When someone has a heart attack, they usually collapse suddenly with a pain in their chest. Some of their heart muscle is not getting enough oxygen, because one of the arteries that supplies oxygen to the heart is blocked by a blood clot. Smoking makes the development of a clot more likely. If the attack is severe, the person may die, but many people survive heart attacks and lead a normal life.

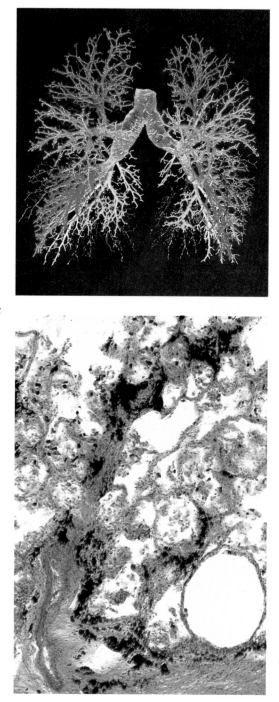

▶ (*top*) Air travels deep inside your lungs through the vast network of passages shown here.
▶ (*bottom*) Smoking damages air passages. Millions of particles of tar are breathed in with each puff of smoke. You can see lumps of black tar in this photo of lung tissue from a cigarette smoker.

Taking good care of your heart and lungs

Your heart and lungs are vital to you. They work tirelessly all your life. Most of the time you don't take any notice of them, but there are some things you can do to keep them healthy.

Watch your diet. If you are overweight, this puts a strain on your heart, since it has more of you to pump blood around!

Some foods, eaten in large amounts over a lifetime, may cause the blood vessels to become clogged. This can cause high blood pressure and heart disease.

▼ For a good diet, you can eat lots of whole foods, fresh vegetables, fresh fruit, and rice. But you should eat less sugar, dairy products, salt, fatty meat, cakes, and chocolate.

You can enjoy lots of . . .

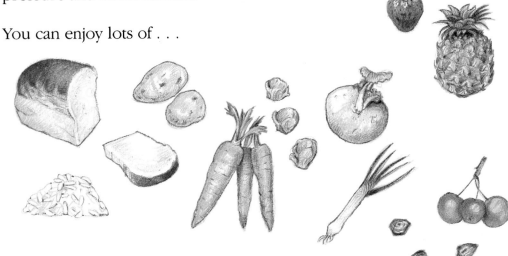

But you should eat smaller amounts of . . .

Avoid smoking. Some adults smoke, even though smoking causes many serious health problems. Others don't want to smoke, but they find it difficult to stop. So it's much better not to start.

Cigarette smoke contains nicotine, tar, and carbon monoxide – all substances that can damage your body.

Smoking paralyzes the cilia that line the air passages, so they cannot properly waft up dust, dirt, and tiny particles of tar. These clog up the lungs and irritate the lung cells, which can make the cells grow the wrong shape. This can lead to the disease called *lung cancer*.

When you breathe in carbon monoxide, it takes up the place in the red blood cells that should be filled with oxygen. This means that your blood won't be taking enough oxygen around your body for it to work at its most efficient level.

Exercise. Regular amounts of moderate exercise will help to keep your heart and lungs fit. Exercise will reduce the risk of heart disease as you get older. Swimming, running, and walking are all good for you.

Glossary

abdomen the area of your body between the bottom of the rib cage and the hip bones, containing internal organs such as the stomach.

alveoli tiny hollow air sacs in the lungs.

aorta the largest artery in the body.

arteries the tubular blood vessels that carry blood away from the heart.

atrium the upper chamber of each side of your heart.

bronchioles small air passages inside your lungs.

bronchus an air tube that leads from the windpipe into the lungs; there are two bronchi, one going into each lung.

capillaries tiny blood vessels.

cardiac muscle a special type of muscle found only in the heart.

cells the tiny living units that make up all the different parts of your body.

cilia tiny hairs or hairlike projections that often help move substances along.

congenital defect an abnormality that you are born with.

cystic fibrosis a disease some people are born with that affects the lungs and digestive organs.

diaphragm the large dome-shaped muscle attached to the bottom of your lungs and used in breathing.

epiglottis the flap which closes over your larynx when you swallow, to stop food from going down into your lungs.

epithelial cells cells which make up the skin and line the inside of your internal organs, such as your stomach.

esophagus the food pipe (upper part of the digestive tract).

hemoglobin the substance in red blood cells that carries oxygen and carbon dioxide around the body.

intercostal muscles small muscles between the ribs which help your chest move in and out.

larynx the lower part of the throat that links the pharynx with the windpipe and contains the vocal cords.

lobes compartments of certain organs and bodily parts, such as the lungs.

lung cancer a disease in which lung tissue produces abnormal cells which form a growth or tumor.

nerve cells the basic units of the nervous system which carry messages between your brain and the rest of your body.

olfactory nerve the nerve that carries messages from the nose to the brain.

pacemaker the group of special cells in the right atrium of your heart that instructs it to beat.

parietal layer (of the pleura) layer which is attached to the inside of the rib cage and diaphragm.

pharynx the top part of the throat between the mouth and the esophagus.

plasma the clear yellow liquid in which blood cells are suspended.

platelets   disklike substances in the blood that help it to clot.

pleura   the membrane which covers your lungs and lines the walls of your chest and diaphragm.

red cells   blood cells which deliver oxygen to and remove carbon dioxide from your body.

scab   a dried-up blood clot on the surface of your skin.

septum   a dividing wall, such as that dividing your nose into two nostrils and your heart into two sides.

small intestine   the part of your digestive system, inside your abdomen, where food is digested.

sphygmomanometer   a machine used to measure blood pressure.

tissues   groups of similar cells joined together for a specific task.

trachea   the windpipe, the main air tube running from the larynx to the lungs.

urine   a liquid produced by your kidneys which contains waste products and water.

valves   flaps in your heart and veins which allow blood to pass onward and prevent it from flowing backward.

veins   the tubular blood vessels which carry blood back to your heart.

ventricle   the lower chamber of each side of your heart.

visceral layer (of the pleura)   layer which is attached to the lungs.

vocal cords   the two soft folds which open and close across the inside of the larynx, making sounds when air passes over them.

white cells   colorless blood cells which help protect the body from infection and destroy unwanted bacteria.

Index